Introduction

Among the "hot issues" of the eighties, the subject of women would certainly rank in the top ten. Words like "feminist," "women's lib," "male chauvinism," and "chairperson" were virtually unheard of a couple of decades ago. No longer. Not only are we learning a whole new vocabulary, we are being introduced to a whole new female identity. Today's woman is refusing to "sit back and shut up" any longer, even though she is still being told to do so . . . often with Bible verses attached.

All the issues on this subject are much too volatile, extensive, and complicated to be solved in a small booklet less than thirty pages long. In no way am I interested in or attempting to address or answer all the questions. You should know that up front before reading any further.

I am a student and teacher of Scripture and by no means an authority on women. I am a happily married husband of one wife (for twenty-eight years), strongly supported and deeply loved. I have no hidden frustration I need to "work through" or some secret message all the world desperately needs to hear. I see wrongs that need to be corrected at both extremes and some long overdue rights that need to be declared when the issues are brought into proper focus. My exposure to the problems has been limited, but my eyes have not been closed to the things I have observed, experienced, heard, and read during twenty-plus years of ministry alongside people, many of whom live in the grays somewhere between bewilderment and deep depression.

I do have one major message I hope to communicate, however. Because it is clearly in need of being proclaimed and because it is so obviously set forth in God's Word, the Bible, I am able to write about it with a great deal of conviction and certainty. It is this, plain and simple: *Women are people of worth and dignity.* I sincerely hope those seven words will come through loud and clear as you weave your way through this booklet.

If you are a woman who is beginning to doubt your value, finding yourself in need of encouragement and affirmation, or if you are a man who tends to relegate women, in general, to a subhuman role (and deep down inside you are honestly starting to wonder if that kind of thinking is more traditional than scriptural), then these pages should help.

Charles R. Swindoll

Woman

The Battle Rages

Extremes fuel the fire of every moment. Push them far enough, scream them loud and long enough, and you've got a revolution on your hands. Like:

"Never believe a woman, not even a dead one." (Old German proverb)

"Woman is a calamity, but every house must have its curse." (Persian saying)

"Do not trust a good woman, and keep away from a bad one." (Portuguese proverb)

"Wives should be kept barefoot in the summer and pregnant in the winter." (Old Deep South philosophy)

Or like:

"Men become older, but they never become good." (Oscar Wilde)

"The libido of the American man is focused almost entirely upon his business so that as a husband he is glad to have no responsibilities. . . . It is what I call the laziness of the American man." (Carl Jung)

"I'm loud, and I'm vulgar, and I wear the pants in this house because somebody's got to. . . ." (Line from "Who's Afraid of Virginia Woolf?")

"If independence is a necessary concomitant of freedom, women must not marry." *(The Female Eunuch,* Germaine Greer)

"The world will not change . . . liberation will not happen unless individual women agree to be outcasts, eccentrics, perverts, and whatever the powers-to-be choose to call them." (Greer)

Those are extreme statements made by men and women alike, with both sexes representing both sides. So-called authorities shout their wares from free-speech platforms, best-selling books, radio and television talk shows, magazines, and movies. While some are subtle, many are overt and brash. They are "experts" playing Pied Piper roles, each extreme with followers by the thousands.

"Whom do I believe? Which do I follow?" There's the "total" woman advocate saying true feminity means "full surrender to your man" . . . but there's also the radical feminist and her ilk who sneer at such "subservient advice," speaking more of absolute equality, female dominance, and assertiveness. Both have success stories to bolster their public image. Both claim a philosophy that works, one that offers answers to the woman who lingers somewhere between feeling forgotten and being frustrated.

Dirty Deals, Independence, Submission, and Other Topics

Not being a woman, I am unable to enter into a soul-level struggle with such warlike propaganda. But I have had opportunity to observe the field of battle and do a little analysis of the situation. Here are some of my observations:

1. Some women today have gotten a dirty deal and have every reason to be angry.

Wife-battering is, for some husbands, a favorite indoor sport. Emotional cruelty and abuse is just as damaging—and far more prevalent than physical mistreatment. Many a fine, faithful wife and mother has been abandoned to make it on her own. She has several small children and no marketable skills. Adding insult to injury, she helped her now-runaway husband through school.

2. Some women lack discernment and clear thinking on today's propaganda from both extremes.

Those who have been ripped off are ready-made shock troops for the woman's lib crusade. What's there to question? She's been shoved down and stomped on long enough . . . and anybody who's willing to champion her cause gets her vote.

Then there is the traditional woman who lived with a dominant dad and a mousy mom, was raised in a culture that frequently tightened the screws on submission—far beyond the biblical bounds—and (naturally) married a guy who wanted a doormat for a wife. She's as gullible to those who demand absolute silence and total submission as her aggressive sister is to the militant message of the feminist leader.

3. As a result, some women have become much more masculine than feminine, unattractively independent, and offensively assertive.

This seems to come with the territory. Whoever buys the line, wears the garb. I know of few things more disgusting, personally, or more fallacious, biblically, than a lovely, feminine, once-attractive lady who has adopted masculine responses and characteristics.

4. On the other hand, some women have begun to blend into the woodwork, mistaking submission as a synonym of spinelessness, passivity, human bondage, and waiting on every whim of her man, with no will of her own.

If you have ever witnessed a lady with this mentality, you've seen a pathetic sight. It's what I call the "whipped dog" look. More often than not, she lives with a frightfully low self-image, wearing an inferior look that announces incompetence, timidity, and fear. To make matters worse, this person frequently lives under the delusion that she is modeling the biblical message. Few things could be further from the truth!

5. Confusion often reigns when it comes to knowing a woman's role and identity according to the Scriptures.

I write that with a sigh, not a frown. It's understandable, since women have so many voices of authority to choose from . . . each inviting "follow me." And so? So they roam from seminar to feminar, conference to congress, book to film series to cassette tape, hoping to find a guru who will solve that gnawing dilemma.

6. In our society today only a few are genuinely satisfied and fulfilled, whether married or single.

Have you ever known a time when more people are less happy? How many do you know who live with someone whom they deeply love, are secure enough to have nothing to prove, enjoy living, and absorb affirmation and security in their home? Precious few. The result is a devastating blow on today's family. You are now somewhat weird if you are happily married (*or* happily single), enjoy children, and appreciate and uphold things like sexual fidelity, long-term commitments, and other facets of the wedding vows.

Driven toward Two Extremes

I could go on, but we need no further evidence. Small wonder *more* women aren't confused. In summary, there are two extremes that have boarded the ship of today's society.

First, there is the overly aggressive woman who is unwilling to be led or reproved by almost anyone, especially a man, and who hates the terms like "submit" or "the woman's place." This person leaves in her wake threatened husband(s), confused and insecure kids, loneliness, isolation, and a variety of offenses.

Second, there is the inordinately passive, intimidated woman who lacks confidence and charm, opinions, and convictions. She is not simply committed to her home, she's *bound* there. The thought of working outside the home is foreign to this lady. She is therefore fairly unaware of the real world beyond her walls, for she is slavishly at the disposal of her husband and chil-

8

dren, cowering and apologetic, forever waiting
to fill no role above that of a silent servant. I find
that this type of woman suffers most disorienta-
tion when (a) the children leave the nest, and/or
(b) the husband dies prematurely and she is
forced to face the blast of hard, cold reality.

The first extreme represents what we might
call a *secular* philosophy of life, while the second
is a *traditional* philosophy. Neither, allow me to
repeat, is appealing *or* biblical. Only a casual
reading of several scriptural passages (for ex-
ample, Proverbs 31, the most detailed and
lengthy portrait of a woman in all the Bible) will
reveal that neither extreme is found in God's
Word . . . unless, of course, the reader reads it
into the text.

What Has Caused Such Extremes?

As we look at these ex-
tremes, a question emerges: Why have we moved
in these directions? What are the causes of such
biblically inaccurate and emotionally unhealthy
extremes? I can think of several causes.

1. A misunderstanding and misapplication of
"submission."

Husbands and wives alike have done this. Pas-
tors and other so-called authorities have also
contributed to this most unfortunate problem.

2. A failure on the part of Christian *husbands*
to carry out three essential responsibilities,
namely:

- to think biblically
- to lead fairly
- to release unselfishly

3. A strong, well-organized action from the secular world system to "liberate" today's woman . . . regardless.

Even those who don't want to be "liberated" are made to appear foolish and backward. The happy homemaker, the fulfilled woman who enjoys being at home is mocked by the system.

4. An equally strong resistance from some voices in Christendom to keep the Christian woman boxed in, seated, and silent.

How Does Scripture Portray the Woman?

Perhaps it's at this point that we need to spend some time. If the Bible does not portray an extreme picture of the woman, what picture does it provide?

I decided to answer that question several months ago. With pencil and paper in hand, I began to turn through the pages of the Bible and take a close, firsthand look at many of the ladies found there. By the time I came to the final pages, I was struck with one overriding thought. Except in a few isolated and special occasions, the women who appear in Scripture are competent, secure, qualified people who had responsible roles to fill and in doing so played a vital part in the shaping of history and in the development of lives. They are beautiful examples of humanity at every economic level of society.

Let me share with you some of the examples I found in my study. But let's limit them to the New Testament and to just a few of the more prominent cases.

● Mary and Martha were close friends of Jesus (Luke 10:38-39).

- Mary anointed Jesus prior to His death (John 12:3).

- Many women lamented Jesus' crucifixion (Luke 23:27-31; John 19:25).

- Women visited Jesus' tomb on resurrection morning (Luke 23:55-24:1).

- Early church leaders responded positively to widows' complaints (Acts 6:1-7).

- Dorcas abounded "with deeds of kindness and charity . . ." (she was extremely well-known in her community) (Acts 9:36).

- The church gathered in Mary's home to pray for Peter (Acts 12:12).

- Jews aroused "the devout women of prominence . . ." against Paul and Barnabas (Acts 13:50).

- Women gathered for worship at Philippi. Paul spoke to them (Acts 16:13).

- Lydia was a successful businesswoman who became a Christian and prevailed upon Paul and his colleagues to meet in her home (Acts 16:14-15).

- In Athens "a number of leading women" were responsive to Paul's and Silas's teaching (Acts 17:4).

- In Athens "many . . . believed, along with a number of prominent Greek women . . ." (Acts 17:12).

- Some believed (still in Athens), including a woman named Damaris (Acts 17:34).

- Aquila and his wife Priscilla were often mentioned (Acts 18:2, 18).

- Paul called these two his "fellow workers" (Romans 16:3).

- Both Aquila *and* *Priscilla* helped hone Apollos's theology (Acts 18:26).

- Paul mentioned Phoebe as "a servant of the church . . . helper of many and of myself as well" (Romans 16:1-2).

- "Chloe's people" gave Paul information on a Corinthian problem (1 Corinthians 1:11).

- Widows were given special attention, assistance, and care (1 Timothy 5:3-16).

- Older women were instructed to "encourage" younger women (Titus 2:4).

- Apphia was called "our sister" in the Philemon letter (Philemon 2).

- The second letter of John was addressed to "the chosen lady . . ." (2 John 1).

Even in this limited and random list, you can see numerous accounts of significant women who occupied places and roles of strategic importance. Frankly, I am convinced this underscores the fact that God never intended the woman to feel inferior or to live fearfully beneath some heavy cloud of unfair domination. While no one who takes Scripture seriously can deny that a wife must, indeed, fit into her husband's plans (1 Peter 3:1) and ultimately allow him the place of final authority in the home (Ephesians 5:22), in no way is she ever viewed as an individual lacking in worth or dignity. Look back over that list and decide for yourself.

Perhaps you have begun to catch a rather bold implication in my comments. The word is *balance.* In my opinion this is one of the clearest marks of maturity a Christian woman can demonstrate today . . . living apart from either extreme, yet fully alive; functioning to her maximum capacity; free to be who she is, yet willing to live within the God-given limits He has prescribed for the home. She doesn't chafe at being a help and an encouragement to her husband. She has few frustrations (aside from those normal to all humanity!) connected with her place in life or her contributions to her world, which is broader, by the way, than the fence surrounding her place of residence.

A Brief Word to Husbands

I sense that some ladies who read these lines are thinking, "Talk to my husband. That balanced role you describe is very appealing to me—something I *long* for—but he can't see it. He's holding me down. I'm not a rebel, but I see the need for broadening my world and finding areas where my self-esteem can be strengthened."

Husband, can you take it straight? I believe you can. You need to take an honest, realistic look at your wife. You also need to hear what she's saying. And why she is saying it. You would do well to imagine yourself in *her* place, for a change (which includes living with you, pal!). Visualize yourself trying to find meaning and purpose in the limited space her responsibilities require of her. Imagine trying to respond to your expectations and demands.

How about a weekend away, just the two of you? How about a long talk? How about soon? Here are a few discussion questions to get the conversation flowing:

- What are some of the things you'd love to do—or become—as a woman that seem impossible right now? Please be specific and open with me.

- Am I sensitive to your deep needs? Are there areas of improvement I could make to give you renewed hope as my wife?

- I want to demonstrate true love to you and to be God's man in our home. In your opinion, is my love freeing or smothering? Am I allowing you room and time to become the woman God would have you to be?

- Love and commitment deepen as two people work toward common goals in a marriage. Let's talk about our goals as husband and wife.

- If something suddenly happened to me, how would you be able to go on? Are we being realistic with inevitable things that will impact our future, like the children leaving the nest or my dying prematurely?

- What are some of your fears? Your hurts? Your frustrations?

- Ever think about walking away from it all? What things can I do to help strengthen your commitment to me and to our marriage?

- On a scale of one to ten (one being the least, ten the most), how would you rank our *relationship?* Why?

Now, friend . . . those are gutsy, let's-not-skate-around-the-block questions. But if you are willing to take that risk and to give your wife the freedom to express herself in those areas, you won't have much trouble knowing the whole truth concerning your marriage. You'll also gain

14

some valuable insights into why things have become so strained under the roof where you live.

Is this kind of thing biblical? I mean, is it part of being a loving husband? Look at 1 Peter 3:7:

> You husbands likewise, live with your wives in an understanding way, as with a weaker vessel, since she is a woman; and grant her honor as a fellow heir of the grace of life, so that your prayers may not be hindered.

Study those words carefully. Read them again in another rendering:

> In the same way you married men should live considerately with [your wives], with an intelligent recognition [of the marriage relation], honoring the woman as [physically] the weaker, but [realizing that you] are joint heirs of the grace (God's unmerited favor) of life, in order that your prayers may not be hindered and cut off.—Otherwise you cannot pray effectively. (From The Amplified New Testament, © 1954, 1958 by The Lockman Foundation. Used by permission.)

Peter's advice could be summarized in three short statements: Dwell with your wife. Know the woman you live with. Give her honor. He's not simply saying eat, sleep, and dress . . . work around the house, and entertain together. He's saying *be* together. Intimately aware and acquainted. Get to know that lady! Discover her. Treat her with respect. Assign honor to her. In my book on marriage[1] I spend considerable time spelling this out. Let me urge you to follow through with your responsibilities before you come down any harder on her to carry out her part of the relationship. 'Nuff said.

A Balanced Woman of God

Ladies, after my scriptural search, I came to three conclusions regarding this matter of being a balanced woman of God. Each will require a good deal of your time and each will call for a fair amount of effort if you hope to put it into action personally.

A balanced woman of God sees Scripture as God's vital and relevant Word worth her attention, devotion, and application.

I learned this principle from Timothy's mother Eunice and his maternal grandmother Lois.

> And he [Paul] came also to Derbe and to Lystra. And behold, a certain disciple was there, named Timothy, the son of a Jewish woman who was a believer, but his father was a Greek, and he was well spoken of by the brethren who were in Lystra and Iconium (Acts 16:1-2).

> I [Paul] thank God, whom I serve with a clear conscience the way my forefathers did, as I constantly remember you [Timothy] in my prayers night and day, longing to see you, even as I recall your tears, so that I may be filled with joy. For I am mindful of the sincere faith within you, which first dwelt in your grandmother Lois, and your mother Eunice, and I am sure that it is in you as well (2 Timothy 1:3-5).

> And that from childhood you have
> known the sacred writings which are able
> to give you the wisdom that leads to
> salvation through faith which is in Christ
> Jesus (2 Timothy 3:15).

On the basis of these biblical examples, I challenge you to get serious about the Bible. Start meeting with God on a regular basis each day. Get away from those hours spent in secular magazines and cheap novels, watching the soaps, and listening to the gossip garbage from neighbors! Become a woman who knows her Bible. You will be amazed at the built-in filter system God's truth will provide.

A balanced woman of God sees herself as valuable, gifted, responsible for her own growth and maturity . . . not overly dependent on anyone to get her through life or to make her secure.

I learned this second principle from a first-century businesswoman named Lydia and the wife of Aquila, a terrific lady named Priscilla.

> Therefore putting out to sea from
> Troas, we ran a straight course to
> Samothrace, and on the day following to
> Neapolis; and from there to Philippi,
> which is a leading city of the district of
> Macedonia, a Roman colony; and we were
> staying in this city for some days. And on
> the Sabbath day we went outside the gate
> to a riverside, where we were supposing
> that there would be a place of prayer; and
> we sat down and began speaking to the
> women who had assembled.

And a certain woman named Lydia, from the city of Thyatira, a seller of purple fabrics, a worshiper of God, was listening; and the Lord opened her heart to respond to the things spoken by Paul. And when she and her household had been baptized, she urged us, saying, "If you have judged me to be faithful to the Lord, come into my house and stay." And she prevailed upon us (Acts 16:11-15).

After these things he [Paul] left Athens and went to Corinth. And he found a certain Jew named Aquila, a native of Pontus, having recently come from Italy with his wife Priscilla, because Claudius had commanded all the Jews to leave Rome. He came to them, and because he was of the same trade, he stayed with them and they were working; for by trade they were tent-makers. . . .

And Paul, having remained many days longer, took leave of the brethren and put out to sea for Syria, and with him were Priscilla and Aquila (Acts 18:1-3, 18; see also Romans 16:3).

Both of these women were extremely competent people . . . persuasive and responsible, yet teachable and gracious. Again, there was balance. And both were keen thinkers. Priscilla joined her husband as they both (!) helped correct Apollos who was soft in one particular area of his theology.

Now a certain Jew named Apollos, an Alexandrian by birth, an eloquent man, came to Ephesus; and he was mighty in the Scriptures. This man had been instructed in the way of the Lord; and being fervent in spirit, he was speaking and teaching accurately the things concerning Jesus, being acquainted only with the baptism of John; and he began to speak out boldly in the synagogue.

But when Priscilla and Aquila heard him, they took him aside and explained to him the way of God more accurately. And when he wanted to go across to Achaia, the brethren encouraged him and wrote to the disciples to welcome him; and when he arrived, he helped greatly those who had believed through grace; for he powerfully refuted the Jews in public, demonstrating by the Scriptures that Jesus was the Christ (Acts 18:24-28).

I'm not saying that these ladies left their husbands (if Lydia was married) to "do their thing," but they were both highly respected by the apostle Paul. I'm confident Apollos was equally impressed.

Lady, stop blaming someone else for your lack of growth! And remember that even though you are joined to your husband as "heirs together," you're not Siamese twins! If you need your husband for security and hope to go on, it's possible that you have assigned him a role that only your Lord should fill. Think about that.

**A balanced woman of God sees the Lord as
her strength, her refuge, and her shield
when things refuse to be resolved.**

I could be tempted to end
this booklet like a fairy tale, promising you that
life will suddenly start changing, that your husband will become all you need during the next
seventy-two hours, or that your world will begin
to blossom like the rose next spring. No way will I
yield to that temptation.

The fact is, you and I know that usually *we*
must change before anyone else will . . . and
even then there's no guarantee. You may live
with a very strong-willed man. He may not be
willing to talk about it any more (you've tried,
haven't you?) to say nothing of reading some
little booklet written by a guy he doesn't know
(who lives in California, no less!).

Well, take hope. In Acts 21:7-14 a group of
people (several of them women) had difficulty
convincing a strong man to change his mind. In
fact, they failed to do so. But rather than fighting
and forcing, they said simply, "The will of the
Lord be done!" (v. 14) and they left the results
with God.

You may need that counsel most of all today.
Please—do not rely on emotional manipulation
or sexual bargaining or threats of leaving. This
is a case for God to handle. "The will of the Lord
be done!" The world says, "Don't be stupid—pull
out. Get even. Fight back. You've come a long
way baby. *Don't give in!* It's high time that man
learned you're NOT GOING TO TAKE IT ANY
LONGER!!"

But if you wish to be a balanced woman of God (one of the world's endangered species), you will resist that advice. You'll remember that the Lord your God points to an alternate route which, by the way, is despised and mocked in the feminist movement. But of far greater importance, it is clearly set forth in the pages of His ageless Book.

The alternate counsel? God urges you to hang in there and let Him work on your behalf . . . to trust in Him and not panic. To stay close to Him and allow Him to sustain you and to nourish you and to be your stability; your thick, comforting shield of protection. To give you the ability to hold up even though the pressure won't go away.

My friend, it is essential that you believe what these pages have been saying. Believe this statement, even though you may not be hearing it from those who live with you in the same house: *You are a person of worth and dignity.* The word is *valuable* . . . you are too valuable for your Savior and Lord to let go of you and to expect you to right all the wrongs. Or to fight your own battles. You've tried too many times already, remember? Now it's time to rely with calm assurance on His all-conquering power. Do that, starting this very moment.

May the Lord our God give you these three things: Great grace to endure without fear, genuine mercy to forgive without resentment, and prevailing peace to continue without doubt.

Dear Father:

How difficult it is to trust You during times of trouble. This problem is magnified when many authoritative voices are telling us not to do this or to start doing that, all of which is counter to Your counsel. But they are close by and You, Lord, seem so far away . . . so slow to work . . . so terribly silent.

Being a woman pulled in various directions is hard enough when things run smoothly. But it gets downright frightening when relationships are strained and our emotions within start screaming for attention. You know how we are, Lord! It seems like everything works against our feeling that we're worthwhile, valuable people. Our heads tell us "Yes," but our hearts often say "No."

We really want to do what's right. Deep within, our greatest desire is to obey Your voice, to walk within the parameters of Your perfect will, even if that means we don't get our way or we can't understand Your plan. It's easy at such times, however, for us to allow fear to come in like the morning frost and blight our faith. When that happens we run to extremes and act immaturely rather than stand firmly within the safe and godly boundaries of balance. We need Your help, Father.

Do give us new measures of grace. And a vast amount of mercy. And Your matchless peace. May those special gifts free us from panic and get us in tune with Your Word so that everything false and phony will be filtered out as discernment replaces gullibility. And may all this give us a maturity that restrains us from embracing error clothed deceitfully in the garb of truth. With quiet confidence we trust You.

In the name of Jesus,

Amen.

[1]Charles R. Swindoll, *Strike the Original Match* (Portland, Ore.: Multnomah Press, 1000).

Additional Reading

1. Deen, Edith. *All the Women in the Bible.* New York: Harper & Row Publishers, Inc., 1955.

2. Elliot, Elisabeth. *Let Me Be a Woman.* Wheaton, Ill.: Tyndale House Publishers, 1976.

3. Getz, Gene. *The Measure of a Woman.* Ventura, Calif.: Regal Books, 1977.

4. Hendricks, Jeanne. *A Woman for All Seasons.* Nashville, Tenn.: Thomas Nelson Publishers, 1977.

5. Horton, Marilee. *Free to Stay at Home.* Waco, Tex.: Word Books, 1982.

6. Karssen, Gien. *Her Name Is Woman*, Book 1 and Book 2. Colorado Springs, Colo.: NavPress, 1975 and 1977.

7. Landorf, Joyce. *Fragrance of Beauty.* Wheaton, Ill.: Victor Books, 1973.

8. Ortlund, Anne. *Disciplines of the Beautiful Woman.* Waco, Tex.: Word Books, 1977.

9. Pape, Dorothy R. *In Search of God's Ideal Woman.* Downers Grove, Ill.: InterVarsity Press, 1976.

10. Swindoll, Luci. *Wide My World, Narrow My Bed.* Portland, Ore.: Multnomah Press, 1982.